Mahogany Eve

ALAN PAYNE was born in Point-à-Pierre, in the south of Trinidad; and has childhood memories of Grenada, Trinidad and Guyana. He came to England when he was nine, crossing the Atlantic on a French liner and arriving in Plymouth. After studying English at Durham University, he taught in secondary schools in Leicestershire; then moved to Sheffield, doing various jobs before returning to teaching. For twenty years, he taught in an infant school, where he shared his enthusiasm for poetry, story-telling and drama with the children. Since retiring he has visited the Caribbean with his wife – and had many memorable encounters – but now feels that Yorkshire is his home.

Mahogany Eve

Alan Payne

smith|doorstop

the poetry business

Published 2024
by The Poetry Business
Campo House,
54 Campo Lane,
Sheffield S1 2EG
www.poetrybusiness.co.uk

Designed & typeset by Utter.
Printed by Imprint Digital

British Library Cataloguing-in-Publication Data.
A catalogue record for this book is available from the British Library.

Smith|Doorstop is a member of Inpress
www.inpressbooks.co.uk.

Distributed by BookSource, 50 Cambuslang Road,
Cambuslang Investment Park, Glasgow G32 8NB.

The Poetry Business gratefully acknowledges the support
of Arts Council England.

Contents

9   The Bocas

10   For the New Baby

12   Grandma

13   Maracas

14   Saddle Road

15   Grand Anse, Grenada

16   Dwellings

17   Capoui Lake

18   Exploring the Orinoco

20   Ramlila

21   Shiva

22   Atlas

23   S.S. Colombie

24   The Touch Line

26   Menu

27   Cinnamon

28   Lights Out

29   Carol Singer

30   Runaway

34   Irises for my Grandmother

37   Invitations

38   The White Lion

39   'Joe's Blues'

40   Meersbrook & Heeley

42   In Conversation

43   Stannington

44   Fathers and Sons

46   Absalom

47   Lennox

48   Port-au-Prince

49   The Coastal Road

50   Higger Tor

51   A Stranger in a Foreign Land

52   Anthurium Lilies

53   Mother

54   Donation

55   Skew Hill

56   A Postcard from Malaga

57   Maps

58   Mount Ballow, Queensland, Australia

59   Hurricanoes

60   The New World

61   Seasoning

62   The Confession

63   The Classicist

64   Stowaway

66   Funeral

67   The Blackbirds of St. Giles

68   Emancipation

69   Bowl

70   Lukasz

72   Marcelo

73   Castaway

74   The African Tragedian

76   A Local Legend

77   Sprinter

78   Service

79   Mahogany Eve

80   Matisse in Suffolk

81   Henry Moore

82 The Goat and the Bishop

83 Evening Glory

84 The Seamstress

86 Home

87 Portrait

88 Tin Bath

89 Sheffield Railway Station, 2007

90 The Black Prince on the River Don

91 Gruissan

92 Setting Sail

93 Notes

96 Acknowledgements

For Lizzie and Edward

The Bocas

Sailing down the islands,
past Gaspar Grande
and Monos
to Chacachacare
and beyond,
passing through
the Dragon's Mouths,
was the journey
I dreamed of taking
when I lay awake,
listening to trains
passing in the night.

For the New Baby

1

When I was born, Grandma Welch
gave me a smocked suit,

a gift from Europe, from those who survived
war after war,

from the Huguenots who settled
in the east end of London,

from a butcher's shop in Holborn,
from Ilford, Charing Cross,

from air-raid shelters, bomb-sites,
the Bible in times of peril.

2

When I was born, Miss Montenegro
gave me a mug and a cup,

a gift from Africa, from those who survived
the middle passage,

from the slaves who stood their ground,
who took to the hills,

from San Juan, Tunapuna,
the heights of El Tucuche,

from the spider stories of Anansi,
Yoruba poems in praise of Ogun.

3

When I was born, John Rampersad
gave me $1 for two bibs,

a gift from India, from those who survived
one ocean, then another,

from the labourers who settled
in the island of my birth,

from San Fernando, Couva,
the Trinity Hills,

from cane-fields, ramshackle shops,
from all the gods in the *Ramayana*.

Grandma

in memory of Lillian Welch

Born in Holborn,
a thirteenth child,
unlucky,
a toddler when you tripped
over that dog, and fell
a full flight of stairs.

A lifetime later, the scar
on your forehead
still showed where the nail
had entered.

Once, in Port of Spain,
I slipped into your room
and watched you wash.

A bowl of water. A jug.

The light in the semi-dark
emanating from within
the kindness
that your body filled.

Maracas

Trinidad

A calypso praises
the perfect shape
of your bay; the long sweep
of the North Coast Road
down from *The Lookout*
with its unaltered views
to that curved beach
where palm trees
luxuriate and a sea-almond
conjures a mid-day shade.

Sixty years ago, you were
my word for *world*.

Inland, you take other forms,
a waterfall marked
with yellow flags
and pools of candle wax;
a valley of sea-green shallows
where hummingbirds vibrate
and bananaquits dart;
a village with a shop
selling bake and shark,
aloo pies, pawpaw.

Saddle Road
Trinidad

Where the road threaded
a tunnelled arch high up
in the Northern Range,
a single lane passing through
the eye of a needle –
nothing now remains
of the saddle

or my grandmother,
buried in Lapeyrouse
in front of a wall
of white-washed stone.
She entered the Kingdom
in the flight
of a frigatebird

and with her memory
intact, the *Southern Cross*,
her father's striped apron,
a season of landslides,
me chasing a butterfly
by the side of the road
to Maracas.

Grand Anse, Grenada

after Merle Collins

Sea,
I love your wish
to absorb the shore,
your longings as you withdraw.
The retreat of sand
under my feet.
The suckle
of shell and toe.
Your salt chastens.
You bring gifts.
Conspire with the sky
to turn the world into a ball,
turquoise to dolphin-blue
to that darker blue
lined with the light
of a shoal of stars.

Dwellings

I remember Tranquillity,
the church on the corner of our road,
funeral hymns, my father's voice,
me on my skates in the sun,
scabs on my knees, cracks in the concrete,
a steel band in the distance.

In his fan-cooled study, my father
works on a sermon for Whit Sunday,
ambling along a print-black avenue
of chapter and verse,
a path for the faithful to follow.
I glide past his window, unseen.

The moon tugs at my father's heart
as he stands on the pavement,
listening for the sound of my skates,
for my breath on the air.
I will lift up mine eyes unto the hills,
from whence cometh my help.

Out of the dark of Port of Spain
comes a familiar figure, his son.

I imagine my father and I on skates,
chatting away, telling stories.
Secluded squares. Deserted boulevards.
No one else in the world.
Bach's *Toccata and Fugue in D Minor*
from within Tranquillity.

Capoui Lake
Guyana

On the edge of the Capoui,
a scattering of huts –
each one as round as a vowel,
hammock-slung, open
to a random air.

The few who remain
give our gazes the slip,
slide into shy smiles,
shuffle into eeriness.

Only one is solid:
a fisherman, who stands,
as if carved out of wood,
a figure on a stamp,
slender spear raised,
eye trained on fish.

Behind him, on the lake,
his ancestors
gather like mist.

Exploring the Orinoco

With the Thames in their hearts,
and childhood fevers in common,
my father and his brother
explored the Orinoco.

The boat of my father's faith
carried them upstream
to the port of Encaramada,
past the granite domes
of Punta Curiquima.

There, on a deserted island,
they camped for the night,
sitting on the scattered husks
of turtle shells,
reading in the moonlight,
and dining. A faint stink
of rotting crocodiles
corroded the air.

During the night, a jaguar
added discord to the howling
of their dogs,
and cataracks answered
the rumbles overhead.

Once, a small black monkey,
like a widow in mourning,
returned the sweet, sceptical smile
of my father's brother
as he glanced up
from his beloved Darwin.
With a pencil, he underlined

a few words; then disappeared
into the forest
of my father's mind,
where their mother's grief
(one boy saved, one lost)
left him bereft.

Ramlila
Trinidad

In a field near Chaguanas,
the *Ramayana* flies its flags.

Arrows rainbow the sky.

Little Raghoo fills his lungs
with sweetness. Spirit-dances
to a tinny music.
He snatches up a mask.
Hey, Raghoo, licks
like fire for you!

Barebacked Rama,
cane-thin Sita,
quivering Lakshman
tip-toe a feathery crowd.
It ripple-glitters
like the sea;
smells of roti, gunpowder.

In the evening, the demon king –
tar paper on bamboo –
bursts into flames.

Saffron tints firefly the sky.

Shiva
Trinidad

You were our brass god,
the handle of the bell my mother rang
when she called me from play.

I imagined you on the veranda,
sitting, cross-legged, composing letters
on my father's typewriter,

or dancing, perfectly balanced,
butterflies at your elbows,
hummingbirds at your fingertips,

turning your head to gaze at me
in the hammock. In that moment
I'd know who you were.

When I strayed into a temple
in the south of the island,
and saw you on the white-washed wall,

an eye in the middle of your forehead,
and a grey-haired pundit shuffling
towards me in ill-fitting sandals,

I wished I'd stayed in the cane-field
with my brothers; longed for home,
and the call of the bell.

Atlas

Trinidad

Mo takes me by the hand,
leads me into a mosque
at the edge of the Gulf.
He whistles. Over our heads
a hummingbird darts,
hovers in front of a flame.

Before I sail for England,
Mo signs my atlas.
In the Atlantic Ocean
he draws a dome,
a sickle moon and a star,
a scarlet ibis returning to land.

S.S. Colombie

Sudden stars pulled us through
the Dragon's Mouths.
Port of Spain extinguished.
Home and homeliness
already a legend.

Next day, briefly ashore
in Guadaloupe –
the patois a distorted version
of a beloved tongue,
its lilt curled in my ear.

Crossing the Atlantic –
a band's orchestrated goodbyes
lost in the wind,
the thundery embrace
of the Northern Range
an echo in the swell,
my stuffed alligator
a talisman.

Fabled Plymouth.
And the journey north, by train,
to Apperley Bridge.
There, in that no-man's-land,
I tasted pickled onions.
Assumed a stranger's skin.
A worsted suit.

The Touch Line

1

He was a reforming minister
who argued
for a liberal reading
of gospel words.

In San Fernando, he visited
workers in the fields
fighting for a fair wage
and union rights.

Massa day dead,
they said. He told them
that the Lord
was on their side.

2

One evening, as hymns
lifted hearts
in Tunapuna, he waved
goodbye to his son –

who boarded a ship
bound for Plymouth,
and a Wesleyan school
on the edge of the moors

where he was frozen
by the banter of other boys.
The headmaster noted:
He can't even dress himself.

3

One of his congregation
accused him
of being a Jesuit.
Others nodded their heads.

Sister Beatrice was ambushed
on the Roosevelt Highway.
His wife retreated to her room.
And then there was his son:

his weekly letters
contained little more
than the loss of a match
observed from the touch line.

Menu

Stereotypical, I know, this woman
carrying an urn on her head, smiling,
as if it's nothing to have walked
to the market in Tunapuna,
and this man who, good-naturedly,
holds out his cup, and this donkey,
waiting patiently by the man's side,
still, with well-behaved ears.

My father framed it, hung it on a wall,
a reminder of *S.S Colombie*,
au revoir, the French waiter
with one blue eye, one green eye,
Trinidad, Martinique, Guadeloupe,
and then the chilly Atlantic.

Cinnamon

Walking across the quadrangle
where the chestnut tree had stood
encircled by a wrought-iron seat,
and where the rope for the bell
which had summoned him
from bed each morning still dangled,
he brushed against a boy
removing his glasses
before being punched –
for liking cinnamon on toast,
for reading *Gilgamesh*,
for not banging his desk-lid
when the 1st XV beat Ashville
by a late dropped goal.

Lights Out

flying fish,
the Azores,
the English Channel

steam and smoke,
green fields,
double-decker buses

fellow-travellers,
suits and hats,
laughter, goodbyes

tiles on the floors,
tiles on the walls,
the smell of beer

platform crowded,
trunk unloaded,
mother stoical

narrow dormitories,
bare classrooms,
Latin

a gap in the wall,
trains speeding by,
the Aire frozen over

a fallen palm tree,
mangroves,
scarlet ibis

Carol Singer

After lights out we have to be silent.
Even so, to be told to go out into the night,
stand in the quad, and sing like the holy
infant, in slippers and dressing-gown, on a night
like this, snowflakes falling on all –
the chestnut tree, the low steps by the door – is
enough to give one the shakes. Stay calm.
Someone will come. Someone benevolent. All
will be well. The clock in the tower is
quiet. Snow slips from the roof. All is not bright.

Runaway

I'm lying on a bed in the sanatorium,
trying to remember my name.

Slowly, things come back to me:
a game of rugby ...
a misty field ...
the Aire ...

A blow to my head.

✳

I am, but I am not of.

✳

For the past five years, every Sunday,
I've written a letter to my parents,
and given it to my housemaster
to read and then post.

This Sunday, I include a quotation
from Jean-Paul Sartre:
Man is the sum of his actions.

✳

At the end of the evening service,
I shove a piece of paper
into the preacher's hand.

TICKET TO HEAVEN

I'm returning the ticket!

*

I ease the key from behind the glass,
unlock the fire-door,
climb down the fire-escape.

My feet on the rungs feel real.

*

Night air and the lights of Bradford.
I set off, up the hill, towards Rawdon.
There's no one about.

*

Near the traffic-lights at Menston,
a policeman stops me,
shines his torch into my duffel-bag:
a Mars bar, a paperback –
The Outsider.

So you're meeting a friend in Ilkley?

He lets me walk on.

*

If I get to the moors, I'll be okay.
A boy without a name
living on rain-water,
roots of heather,
memories of the Caribbean.

The air will be warm
above initialled rocks.

＊

By the time I reach Burley-in-Wharfedale,
part of me is thinking about
Existentialism and Humanism,
and part wondering
if it wouldn't be wiser
to turn back.

＊

My first night away from home.

I've already forgotten
if my father said goodbye
to me or not,
but see my mother
not seeing me
when she said goodbye.

I've already been told
that whatever I ask for
the answer will be no;
and to wash the Brylcream
out of my hair
before my head

touches the pillow.

＊

On Leave Days,
I shake hands with my father,
remain aloof from my mother.
Sometimes call her *Matron*.
A slip of the tongue.

*

I am, but I am not of.

*

The following morning I'm summoned
to the office. I imagine the scene:
the two secretaries, the headmaster,
the policeman who took my details.

I push open the door.

My housemaster is there, genial
as ever, with a new boy
of about my own age.

This is ...

We glance at each other.

He's from Barbados.

We shake hands.

*I'd like you to look after him,
make sure he's okay.*

Irises for my Grandmother

in memory of Elizabeth ('Bessie') Alice Payne

March 2016

Propped against a cup,
a postcard of a single iris,
painted in 1610,
a symbol of faith.

August 1966

On a warm Sunday evening,
after church, after whist,
my father slipped me an envelope.
My mother said: *It's for you.*
Grandma's engagement ring.

A trinity of diamonds brought back
her best Sunday dress, its crinkly sheen,
hymns round the piano,
the letters she wrote.
My dearest –

July 1959

An airmail from Essex.
The familiar handwriting,
thin blue paper, darker blue of the ink ...
wrinkly skin, arthritic hands.

My father cleared his throat,
read aloud: *Grandpa can't wait
to see the boys.
Of course, you'll all miss*

the Caribbean.
Grey skies instead of blue!

And then, after the heart-ache
of leaving Port of Spain,
seeing her in her garden,
standing next to a clump
of her favourite flowers.
Look at the irises!
Such a lovely blue!

December 1961

After hearing me practice
my scales and arpeggios,
she gave me a hymn book,
one with tunes.

She read from the Preface:
'Methodism was born in song.'
Her voice warm as cocoa.
We've never ceased to sing!

October 1965

Hands a-tremble, she arranged
neat columns of cards on the table,

told me something I didn't know:
my father had an older brother

called John, after John Wesley.
He was only four when he died

of diphtheria. 1st June 1916.
My heart aches for him still.

July 1966

The last day of term:
informed of her death
by my housemaster

... kept from me
so I could concentrate
on my exams.

Her funeral missed
so I could brush up
on Caesar's Gallic Wars.

May 2016

Irises for my grandmother,
fifty years too late.
I place them in a vase
by the window.

Invitations

A woman's face blossoms
at the door of
the Ruskin Museum.
Genevieve Pilley,
curator, artist,
flanked by two peacocks,
invites us in.

You too, she says,
can follow your heart
along Brook Road,
then step into
the Piazza San Marco,
where the pigeons wait,
patiently, to be drawn.

Leaves, feathers, rocks,
the coloured letters
of an illuminated page,
Turner's painting of Sheffield,
are all invitations
to look out of the window
and see what's there.

The White Lion
Sheffield

A stained-glass window:
WINDSOR ALES

Below, a thin man
with a pile of marking

juggles apostrophes,
while all about him

lovers meet for the first time,
decide to give it a go

over a pint of bitter,
a half of lager.

Punctuation matters.
Beyond the window, snow.

'Joe's Blues'
Sheffield

A concrete yard,
two rabbits in a hutch,
men in sharp suits,
one of them saying, *Maybe* –

An introduction to Chico,
a laconic *Hey* –

A wood-burner, bare walls,
cans on a table,
a thin woman, smoking

A girl in a low cut dress
throws away her crutch,
dances close

The smell of her hair

This is it, this is life –

Meersbrook & Heeley

From the top of the park
nothing marks their houses;
no shadows
darken their walls,
sink holes
into windows.
All had addresses.

One hanged himself
in the gulley –
from the branch of a tree
where children
looped a rope
to swing out
over the dried-up brook.

Another known only
by the number
on his door
shook his head
when he walked
a thin dog
and muttered.

And one with dreadlocks
who talked
to Bob Marley
was driven
from his flat
by the voices
in his head.

All had their reasons.
Nightly, a light
shone on a landing.
He was a closed book,
we said, looking away,
towards other streets,
other neighbourhoods.

In Conversation

Harold Pinter at the Crucible Theatre, Sheffield

Hands grip crook of walking-stick.
You sit. Spot-lit.
Rasp of tongue on teeth.
Voice elegantly wrecked.

You pause. We wait.
A flick of your wrist releases dove after dove,
flights of rant, riffs gentle as mist,
brutal as a tomahawk blow.

How are you?

Your hands pirouette.

Stannington
near Sheffield

In his tartan shirt, the farmer's lad passes,
turning his back on his father's sheep,
his father's cows, his father's acres,
his mother singing hymns while pegging washing on the line.

He slouches past the dog flattening her belly on the ground,
the chapel where he broke a window,
the gate where he saw the pastor kiss a man in the rain,
his grandfather's grave, with its mound of earth.

In her Sunday School hat, his sister watches him slope off,
on the move, like the moon,
his name tattooed on the nape of his neck.

Fathers and Sons
from V. S. Naipaul

I

At three in the afternoon, when school was over, Anand walked down Victoria Avenue, past the big yellow house where I used to live, past Tranquillity Methodist Church*, past the racketing wheels and straps of the Government Printery,* a metallic choir sometimes joined by the sound of the rain, *crossed Tragarete Road for the shade of the ivy-covered walls of Lapeyrouse Cemetery,* where my grandmother is buried, and turned into Philip Street, where I swapped marbles with a friend in the dusty yard of Miss Richie's one-room school.

II

When Anand won an exhibition place, he walked past *the Scottish baronial castle, the Moorish mansion, the semi-Oriental palace, and came to the blue and red Italianate college* – where soon he would go. He stared at these *architectural marvels,* as I often did, and gazed across the Savannah where one afternoon he allowed me to mount the bicycle he'd been given by his father and ride off into the distance. It was a Royal Enfield, and had belonged to Mr Biswas himself. In the end I dumped it on Frederick Street.

III

In a nondescript room in Queens Park Hotel, at the top of Victoria Avenue, Mr Biswas and my father are sitting at either end of a table, Mr Biswas in front of his yellow typewriter, my father in front of his ancient *Corona.* Mr Biswas is typing a government report, my father working on a Good Friday sermon. Somehow I know that Mr Biswas is thinking about Anand, and my father is thinking about me. Mr Biswas says *I have missed his childhood.* My father solemnly nods his head. For a few moments their fingers are quiet.

IV

Both Anand and I went to England, Anand to university, me to boarding-school. *Mr Biswas missed Anand and worried about him. He wrote Anand long humorous letters.* When the replies came, they were *impersonal, brief, empty, constrained.* Mr Biswas continued to act as *the comforter.* His last letter was *full of delights.* My father's letters were full of regrets. He confessed that he had missed much of my childhood. But he remembered me pulling him out of bed in Guyana when he and I went for an afternoon swim.

Absalom

Briefly, he remembered plunging
through a cascade of trees,
Raleigh bike bucking a jig –
above him monkeys
clattering the light –
until a sudden, slow-motion jam
left him dangling –
hair caught in tree,
each lock hooked by a leafy claw.

And on the edge of the Savannah,
his father's voice.

O Absalom, my son, my son.

Lennox
Grenada

After the hurricane,
my father's friend leans across a table
in a roofless house on Market Hill,
and strokes my father's arm.

He looks out of a hole
where shutters once hung
at a seaplane landing in the harbour,
bringing mail, bringing medicines.

In the tiny playground
of Aunt Etty's one-room school,
children climb on a fallen tree
to watch the seaplane take off.

Your skin is white, Lennox says,
but your heart is black!

Port-au-Prince
Haiti

My father adjusts his pince nez,
gives the correct answers at the airport,
relieved when the suitcase he lost
in Guadeloupe is returned to him.

Driven to a house, he spends the night
listening to insurrectionists.
Political quotes. Wesleyan hymns.
Tomorrow we'll commune with the dead.

In the market, an iron roof magnifies the heat.
A woman on stilts, face painted blue,
leans down, breathes on my father,
leaves her scent on his jacket.

In the cathedral, the bishop instructs him
in the mysteries of Vodou.
Tontons Macoutes, in dark glasses,
watch from the choir stalls.

In his suitcase, wrapped in a shirt –
a mahogany carving of The Last Supper:
bottles of rum, slices of watermelon,
a bullet hole in Christ's side.

The Coastal Road

The panther that padded along
by the side of my father's car
was later caught and killed.
But maybe its breath
and the moist fur of its coat
still shadowed my father's thoughts
like the life he might have had
if it hadn't been too late.

And when, on Kinder Scout,
I follow a hint
at the edge of sight,
scour hollows for tracks,
or stand, hunched,
beneath a sandstone skull –
I too experience an ache
in my aging flesh. Regret.

Higger Tor
Derbyshire

There's a trace of blue
above Higger Tor,
where my father lopes
through layers
of cloud,

a reassurance
on days like this
when I'm missing my son
and winter's dislocations
threaten the heart.

A Stranger in a Foreign Land

When my mother looked in the mirror, she saw, standing behind her, Ruth the Moabite. She heard her voice. *For whither thou goest, I will go, and where thou lodgest, I will lodge.* Ruth had been with her since she'd arrived in Trinidad, been reunited with my father on the veranda of a house in Port of Spain, lodged with some folk in San Fernando, married my father in his church in Princes Town. Ruth was with her when she walked out of the house, when people stared at her, when children touched her skin, wondering what it was like to be white, when she entered the dark of a shop, when she passed walls with murals of gods and goddesses whose names she did not know. Ruth was with her when people wanted to know about London, and she told them about the Blitz, about air-raid shelters, about her train journey to Glasgow, about the *Maaskirk*, about the convoy, about crossing the Atlantic, about her fear of U-boats. And Ruth was still with her, when she drove with my father past cane fields, through Indian Walk, Tableland, Sixth Company, when she was enveloped by smells, burnt sugar, kerosene lamps, Indian cooking, when she missed her cat, when she took class meetings for women.

The Book of Ruth.

Anthurium Lilies

As a child I was encouraged
to marvel at waxy replicas –
pink-faced angels standing
in two brass vases –
rather than *the real thing*
growing in the pagan air
of Trinidad's perpetual fire.

Yet in the labile oils
of the still-life painting
hanging on a wall
of my mother's widowed flat,
flushed, fleshy pinks
invoke a sensuality
as vibrant as steel drums
in the days before
Ash Wednesday.

Mother

It might have been kinder to say:
Yes, all's set, cases packed,

the dark outside your window
the hull of a boat,

lights like the lights of a city
seen through a scattering of trees,

steward already preparing
to meet your needs,

ahead, horizons,
flying-fish, the Trinity Hills.

But you lay in your bed,
lost beneath the glare,

One Thousand Short Stories
abandoned on the floor.

In the morning I woke to a lack;
your body tidied away.

A few boxes for your things:
pictures, books, bundles of letters.

Your voice in my head:
Is the boat here?

Are we ready for going?

Donation

my mother's gift to medical science

Your body still itself, neither ash nor earth,
still one with all the vowels and consonants
of Cranbrook Wash, Stanford Rivers, Havering-atte-Bower.
And one with *Violet*, your middle name.

From your washed-out limbs, organs, arteries
students will learn to look.
Even your blind eye has something to teach.

Cheeks scooped out.
Fingers ringless. Nails chipped.
Toes, serenely awry, mangled by cheap shoes.

A stubbornness in your parted lips.

Skew Hill
Sheffield

My mother's ashes
scattered
between
flinty showers;
a resolution
at last
of all
that reaching out
towards others.

Her desire
to be *useful*
shrunk
to a circle of roses
whose petals
shake themselves free
of the loss
that shapes
a man's bent back
in a field
stunned by rain.

A Postcard from Malaga

You're dead, I know, but still
I'd like to send you *this*:
an old woman, small, stout,
dressed in black,
carrying a bag full of oranges
and a sheaf of flowers
pausing for breath
in the Alcazaba.

Her face shifts and slides –
one ear floating in her hair,
the other hanging
from her chin.

In her I see *you*, your Huguenot genes
replaced by Moorish blood,
a Spanish widow with one eye
staring straight out,
the other
fixed on Our Lady of the Snows,
a Hindu goddess, hand stretched out,
offering an orange
as perfectly formed
as the sun.

Maps

It's not on the tourist route,
but there are always queues
outside this house
where a great cartographer
lived and worked

but never left his room,
preferring the company of parchment
and the glimpse of a bird
on the cathedral spire

to *America Meridionalis*,
Mare Pacificum,
Rio de la Plata,
Terra Australis Incognita,
or *Paradisus*.

Mount Ballow, Queensland, Australia

in memory of Robert Payne

Cousin, you're here, in the mist,
as the south shrinks
to an Antarctic beech, whose leaves
ache with longing for sisters
in Chile and Tierra del Fuego.

You're elsewhere too, in the dark,
as the north contracts
to an Arctic fox, whose young
rustle in an underground den,
unaware of the way continents split.

Hurricanoes

The morning after the storm,
I wheeled my brother-in-law
to the window of the library,
pointed to where a tree
had fallen in the car park,
talked about the wind
that had raged that night.

He seemed to understand.
It was difficult to be sure.
But when I quoted lines
from *King Lear: Blow, winds,*
and crack your cheeks!
Rage! Blow! You cataracts –
he broke into a rueful smile.

The New World

Under the sway
and creak
of sail and rope,
salt-stiff sacks jut
like ruffs
from the necks
of urns
nestling
in the hold.

Stowed away,
like earthy lights,
the first potatoes
to be shipped
shift
in their skins,
anticipating
frost.

Seasoning

Bunce Island, Sierra Leone

The agent spices his day
with antelope, wild boar, river fish,
backgammon, golf with his guests,
bottles of wine from the ice-box,
a visit, maybe, to the hut
in the women's yard,
then relaxing in the orchard
as the sun goes down.

Meanwhile, across the ocean,
new arrivals are being shown
another order of seasoning:
insults, beatings,
a calibrated programme
whose aim is to break their spirits.

The Confession

The day after his wife was cremated,
he summoned his mistress,
met her at the airport,
told his chauffeur to drive them home.

He needed her to answer the door,
manage his diet,
dispose of coats, dresses, underclothes,
comfort him when he scattered the ashes.

One evening, she placed a bowl of salad
on the table. *You'll like this.*
His hands shook
as he hurled it at the fireplace.

He confessed to the gardener
that he saw his wife every day,
behind the pavilion;
charcoal eyebrows, a purple kimono.

The Classicist

She was charmed by the man who came
to her father's house, showed her

how to crack a whip. His voice so gentle.
Scholarly quotes. A twinkle in his eye.

Later the shock of hearing him speak
of the black man having the whip hand

over the white man. His foreboding.
The river Tiber foaming with much blood.

Stowaway

Voices probed the hold,
their calls echoing
like a colony of birds.
Is there anyone there?
Miss Coverdale
and her blind companion
tilted their heads.
We won't hurt you!
A shadow drifted,
then edged upwards –
a child coaxed
into the light.

You can speak to us,
the blind one said.
And Miss Coverdale,
under her breath:
He's nobbut
skin and bone.

A man with a face
pitted and cracked
like the moon
handed him a telescope,
loosening the strings
that kept him taut.
The circle
showed him a bird
above the swell,
and, close-up, passengers,
with rugs and books,
lining the decks.

Off North Carolina,
a flint-voiced colonist
offered 500 bucks
for the boy.

The Captain glanced
at the sky. *Bo'sun,*
he said, *could you use
a young 'un?*

Funeral
Jamaica

In a coffin
a woman places
a chain,
a pair of shackles,
an iron collar,
a whip.

Many voices
raised in song
near William Knibb's
Baptist chapel,
as the coffin
is lowered.

In the dawn light
a mason
from San Domingo
carves on a stone:
Captain Slavery
died 31st July 1838

The Blackbirds of St. Giles

A Georgian ghost of flesh and bone,
he drifts along the Strand,
vanishes in the Embankment's mist,
whistles for luck on Tower Hill,
hears a voice like a wisp of smoke:
The blackbirds of St. Giles are here to stay.

Coachmen, pageboys, bandsmen,
bargemen on the Thames, some on the run,
they meet in *The Yorkshire Stingo*,
play violins, French horns, drums.
Even so, in the street, a few are seized,
betrayed by the scars on their faces.
Bundled onto a ship, they disappear.
Sometimes they sing. Sometimes they don't.

He's given a trumpet concealed in a shirt,
on a whim travels north,
plays African fanfares to celebrate
Evensong, christenings, marriages.
On the outskirts of York, a second gift:
a woman's embrace in the night.
He's with her now, for life.

Emancipation
Trinidad and Tobago

In the days before Carnival,
we gather in Woodford Square
to hear a small man in dark glasses
talk about our island's past.

Massa day gone! Time now
for a political awakening!
Massa day gone! Time now
for a social revolution!

As he talks, other things fall away:
a house fire in San Juan,
the loss of an engagement ring
on the beach at Maracas,

an East Indian journalist fired
from the *Trinidad Guardian*,
the moment, in Laventille,
Beatrice heard an angel speak.

Barefoot man! Time now
for a social revolution!
Barefoot man! Time now
for a political awakening!

On a wall of the Red House
a shy youth daubs *Vote P. N. M.*
And on the Savannah a child sings:
Yankee gone an' Sparrow take over now!

Bowl

This bowl has been passed from hand to hand
for eight hundred years; whoever holds it
hears the song the potter heard
when he made it for his daughter's wedding.

This bowl has been passed from hand to hand
for eight hundred years; whoever holds it
hears the song the potter heard
when he made it for a barefoot traveller.

This bowl has been passed from hand to hand
for eight hundred years; whoever holds it
hears the song the potter heard
when he made it for his son's departure.

A song of home. A song of Syria.

Lukasz
Sheffield

On his first day
at school, Lukasz
hid under a table;
wouldn't come out.

On his second day
at school, he did
the same.

On his third day,
he spotted a tractor
on a shelf –

He pointed.

Mrs Fine, his teacher,
took the tractor
off the shelf,
and held it up.

Lukasz came out,
and his teacher
placed the tractor
in his hands.

Tractor.

He looked at her;
then opened
his mouth –

Tractor.

One day he'd tell her
about the tractor
on his uncle's farm
in Poland.

But not yet.

For the moment,
one word
was enough.

Marcelo

otherwise known as The Chilean

His father bred horses, and in his village
he was known as an accomplished rider.

When he came to Spain, he sent money,
waited for his family to join him.

At first, letters from dear Isabela,
drawings from Fabio. Then nothing.

No wife, no children, no grandchildren.
But he keeps a horse on his balcony.

A marvel on the third floor of a building
in a narrow street where caged birds sing.

Castaway
Derek Walcott

The shock of the familiar
in those lines where you name
the districts of Port of Spain:
Belmont, Woodbrook, Maraval,
Laventille, home of Our Lady,
home of the Desperadoes,
a place of dubious pilgrimage,
standpipes like simple crosses.

I look out of the window and see
a rum-soaked artist at an easel,
a wayward singer in a straw hat,
a fisherman mending his net,
Robinson Crusoe, Man Friday,
a castaway with a furrowed face.

The African Tragedian
Ira Aldridge

A glance into the wings
shows him men shackled
at bone and tongue
shuffling along a plank
towards a ship's
distant hold.
His ear hears their groans.

Yet night after night
he plays to packed houses
in Bristol, Crakow, Cologne.
Othello, *sold to slavery*.
A sympathetic Shylock
asking, *If you prick us,
do we not bleed?*
Princes and kings.

A young Stanislavski,
in neat spectacles,
notes *an eloquence
rooted in
dispossession*,
marks how gently
he breathes his lines.

Is black so base a hue?

In balcony and stalls,
they watch and listen:
a lover from Ireland,
a gravedigger from Lodz,
a serf from the Ukraine.

And here, unremarked,
an artist who captures
(sketchbook on knee)
moonlight in the creases
of a plain white shirt;
that slantwise look
of a man who has travelled
such desperate roads.

A Local Legend

I know a man who runs every day,
a tarmac addict, a city eccentric,
on the back of his faded track suit
a legend: URBAN AND SOBER.

He's been passing *The Fox and Hounds*
and *The Crown* for twenty-five years,
ever since he left a bottle of Guinness
outside *The White Lion*.

He draws pictures of scenes he's seen on the streets,
gives them away to rough sleepers,
children playing truant, refugees,
anyone, like him, running for their lives.

Sprinter

He won every race he entered;
raised a gloved fist
when crossing the line –
for the wretched of the earth.

Accused of ingratitude
by his headmaster,
he chalked on a wall
by the school gate:

>   *INGRATITUDE*
> *IS THE FIRST VIRTUE*
>   *OF REVOLUTION*

He might have written a book
on his hero, Thomas Paine,
become an activist,
figured in an Olympic final.

At nineteen, he suffered
an epileptic fit.
On his coffin lay his spikes,
and a copy of *Rights of Man.*

Service

Serena Williams

Forget the racket,
forget the ball in the air,
forget her hands,
forget the baseline,
forget the clay,
forget her feet.

Study her profile,
her raised eyes,
her chin, mouth, forehead,
the definition of her headband.

It's all there.

A portrait
of the Madonna
at prayer.

Mahogany Eve
from Edna Manley

She glances over her shoulder,
eyes fixed on scenes
beyond the watercolour
of warships passing
Bell Rock in 1940:
U-boats in cold waters,
the *Maaskirk* steaming
across the Atlantic,
my father a passenger,
above and below deck
the darkness lit by men's voices
singing and talking –
ahead of them, a coastline,
and all the islands
of the Lesser Antilles.

Matisse in Suffolk
from Blue Nude IV

Sitting in a canvas chair,
he cuts a dozen shapes
out of the sea and the sky
with a pair of shears.
In his mind, even the gulls
on the water are blue;
blue, too, the pine cones
scattered under his table.

He arranges the shapes:
the shingle at Orford
framed by a window;
three fishing boats;
a woman, sitting, head
tilted forward, reflecting
on the spaces between
one thing and another.

Henry Moore
Perry Green, Hertfordshire

In homely charcoal, sketch after sketch
render forms he's loved for a life-time:
reclining figures, truncated landscapes –
pitted, riven, cored.

Every so often his nurse wheels him
into a different patch of air,
aligns him with a favoured tree.
His breath nuzzles an alternative bronze.

I could stay out here for ever.

The Goat and the Bishop
from Johannes Beerstraten

The goat pulling the sledge
on which the bishop sits
like a mediaeval jester
is in no mood for deviating
from the route across the ice
which leads to the cathedral,

is in no mood for admiring
skaters skating
for the sheer fun of it
on a Sunday morning
when the crisp, clear air
is a temptation in itself,

arrives at the cathedral
in good time, only to find
that the bishop lingers
by the porch, talking
to the beggars and strays
who huddle round a fire,

and later, in his sermon,
much to the goat's disgust,
produces from beneath
the edge of the pulpit,
a pair of skates, and takes
these as his text.

The delights of skating,
the bishop says,
are a foretaste of Paradise.

Evening Glory
from Charles Monkhouse

All day, sky smouldering,
the moon on the full.
Now this:
on the Old Man of Coniston,
a necklace of lights –
a hillside welcome
for Rama and Sita
stepping ashore
in scarves and cagoules.

Awaiting them,
two coppery women
with nothing between them
but a plate
of cassava-cakes.
Their voices flicker.
Manioc, they say.
A gift from Yocahu.

Watching the lake's
elongated lights,
Rama and Sita
share a joke
with the women,
ask them about
Arawakan customs,
cassava-cake crumbs
on their lips.

The Seamstress
Trinidad

She's been waiting
fifty years for him
to return. The galvanize
above her head
a steel-pan ping-pong,
door ajar, hands busy
with stitching the heart's
landscape, a gulley
in Laventille, the beach
at Mayaro.

Outside, a poinsettia
samples a breeze
from the Gulf of Paria –
where she's conjured
a space for him,
a yellow house, on stilts,
roof as blue as the sky,
verandas and jalousies
a fretwork of clouds.

A stick announces
his arrival.

The needle in her hand
is threaded with the song
of a bird, and in her lap
scarlet ibis fly in
to roost.

She hears her son ask,
in his hesitant way
Can I help you?

And a voice as familiar
as San Juan ripens
to a mango red

This is my home.

Home
Trinidad

The pair of us, in the heat,
standing on the pavement,
gazing at the house
that's no longer there,
its yellow walls, veranda,
hanging baskets
from behind which Isabel
appears, in her apron,
a yam in her hands,
above her, a bookcase,
cobwebs descending
from an illustrated edition
of Grimm's Fairy Tales,
a snakeskin on a table,
cracks in the floorboards,
an open window,
me looking down at us,
the pair of us, in the heat,
standing on the pavement,
gazing at the house
that's no longer there.

Can I help you?

Who's this?

A stranger.

What can I say?

This is where we live.

Portrait

The many shades of grey
in a grandmother's hair,
stroked by the sun,
buffed by the moon,
the greys of a westerly sky
beyond the Preseli Hills.

The many songs she mimes
in the mirror, when no one
is looking: *Hey Jude,*
hair black as vinyl,
mouth like a penny.

The many ways in which
she shows her love:
mixing bowl, wooden spoon,
the making of a wish,
the slow geometry
of a patchwork quilt.

Tin Bath

Is good with air.
Will hold it, respectfully,
for many hours,
many years,
if need be, centuries.

Is good with water.
Bare-armed mothers
scrubbing the backs
of husbands,
sons and daughters.

Is good with earth.
Will allow itself
to be filled,
then, in time,
field a company of flowers.

Is good with fire.
A few logs all it takes.
A circle of friends
warming themselves
in a September garden.

Sheffield Railway Station, 2007
Olaudah Equiano

He emerges from beneath the arch,
burnt flesh beneath neat clothes.
Before him, a wall of water
curves like a bone –

fear in the hold,
bodies coffined in rows,
random, muzzled shrieks,
men whipped for refusing to eat.

A skewed figure mouths
I am a man. He knows
how it feels to be robbed
of his name,

and find it again
in the breath on his lips.

The Black Prince on the River Don

Robert Wedderburn

At night, like knotweed,
the dead crowd these banks.
A tailor with pamphlets in his pocket
watches moonlight stitch one weir
to another, sees in a silt island
the shape of Jamaica.

The Don gives him his grandmother,
flogged for raising a storm with
ear of cat, eggshells, fishbones –
her crime, obeah.

The spaces under the arches echo
with her voice, Abyssinia Bridge
resounding with, *Remember boy,*
you baptised in the English church,
but we spirit African.

Under a concrete archway,
The Black Prince daubs words on walls:
Am I Not A Man And A Brother?
in thick white paint.

He knows that soon
the wild figs by this river
will be joined by colonies of mangoes,
bananas, guavas and breadfruit –
each tree fulfilling a radical rhetoric.
And on the banks of the Don
the kingfisher and the hummingbird
will dazzle the light.

Gruissan

the south of France

Commemorating
all those lost at sea,
the blue-world window
harbours an altar
towards which, in the dark,
a prayerful boat sails.

Hear me when I call.

An enclosed sea sweeps in.
December's breakers
push against a wind
that flays the shell
off a crab
and backcombs the spray.

In the *etang*, flamingos,
like novice seers,
shift, uneasily, from foot
to foot. Hear,
in the wind-surge,
rumours of *whatsoever*
passeth through
the paths of the sea.

Setting Sail

Let the boat be piloted
by a man from Carriacou.

Let the hold be lined
with the Old Testament.

Let her sail down the islands,
through the Dragon's Mouths.

Let the sun lose its shape
near Chacachacare.

Let the clouds pass
in gilt-edged robes:

my mother, my father,
the living, the dead.

Notes

The Bocas

The Dragon's Mouths (Bocas del Dragón) is the name of the series
of straits separating the Gulf of Paria from the Caribbean Sea, and
Trinidad from Venezuela. Gaspar Grande, Monos and Chacachare are
small islands to the north-west of Trinidad.

Grand Anse, Grenada

Inspired by 'Sea', a poem by the Grenadian poet Merle Collins, from her
collection *Lady in a Boat*.

Exploring the Orinoco

A few of the details are taken from an abridged translation of Alexander
Von Humboldt's *Personal Narrative of a Journey to the Equinoctial
Regions of the New Continent*, completed in 1834.

Fathers and Sons

The quotations in this prose poem are from V. S. Naipaul's novel, *A
House for Mr Biswas*.

Seasoning

The main details are taken from *Black and British: A Forgotten History*,
by David Olusoga.

Funeral

From *Black and British: A Forgotten History*, by David Olusoga.

The Blackbirds of St Giles

From *Black and British: A Forgotten History*, by David Olusoga.

Emancipation

The 'small man in dark glasses' is Dr Eric Williams, leader of the People's
National Movement, who became the first Prime Minister of Trinidad

and Tobago. The line the child sings is from Mighty Sparrow's calypso *Jean and Dinah*, a big hit in 1956.

Lukasz

Inspired by an anecdote in *The Place That Knows Me*, a memoir by Richard Hines.

Castaway

The poem alludes to *The Castaway and Other Poems*, one of Derek Walcott's early collections.

The African Tragedian

Some of the details are taken from *Ira Aldridge: Celebrated 19th Century Actor*, by Martin Hoyles. The artist in the poem is James Northcote, whose painting of Aldridge, entitled 'Othello, the Moor of Venice', is on display in Manchester Art Gallery.

Sprinter

The poem alludes to Frantz Fanon's classic of anti-colonialism, *The Wretched of the Earth*. The quotation in the middle of the poem is from Thomas Paine.

Mahogany Eve

Edna Manley's mahogany sculpture, 'Eve', is part of the permanent collection in the Graves Art Gallery, Sheffield. Edna Manley was an influential artist in Jamaica. Also part of the collection is a watercolour by Eric Ravilious, painted in 1940, 'Passing the Bell Rock'.

The Goat and the Bishop

Inspired by 'Skaters on the Y in Front of the Paalhuis and the Nieuwe Brug in Amsterdam', painted in 1660 by Jahannes Beerstraten. Among the figures on the ice there's a goat pulling a sledge.

Evening Glory

Inspired by an installation by Charles Monkhouse, a chain of thirteen lights around the summit of The Old Man of Coniston. It was called

'Evening Glory', and was part of the FRED Festival of Site Specific Art 2005. Manioc is another word for cassava, and is of Amerindian origin. Yocahu is the name of an Arawak male god, who is the giver of manioc.

Sheffield Railway Station, 2007

In his *Interesting Narrative*, published in 1789, Olaudah Equiano recorded his kidnapping and subsequent years as a slave, and his eventual road to freedom in the Caribbean and in England. 2007 saw the 200th anniversary of the Slave Trade Act, which prohibited the slave trade in the British Empire, although it did not abolish slavery as such.

The Black Prince on the River Don

Some of the details are taken from *The Axe Laid to the Root: The Story of Robert Wedderburn*, by Martin Hoyles.

Setting Sail

Carriacou is a small island north of Grenada. It has a long tradition of boat building.

Acknowledgements

Acknowledgements are due to the editors of the following, in which some of these poems first appeared: *The North, Smiths Knoll, Scintilla, The Result Is What You See Today: Poems about Running, CAST: The Poetry Business Book of New Contemporary Poets*, Radio Sheffield, *Writing on Air* – a BBC anthology. Also, collections published by *The Word Train: Objects in Art, Relative Values, Cardinal Points, Archipelago, Zigano*. In 2003 'Anthurium Lilies' won second place in the Hilda Cotterill Poetry Prize, judged by Ray Hearne. *Mahogany Eve* includes poems published in *Exploring the Orinoco*, a winner of the Poetry Business Competition in 2009/10, judged by Andrew Motion.

Thanks to the many friends and workshop colleagues who have responded to drafts of these poems; to Ann and Peter Sansom of The Poetry Business; and to Nancy Durham for the photograph on the cover. Special thanks to two of my oldest friends, Roger Hubank and Nick Rogers, and to my wife, Lynne.